Verbal
Reasoning

Fantastic Home Learning

CONTENTS

1 HIDDEN WORDS

A common verbal reasoning question is the 'hidden words' question. In this question, at least two words are given and you must find a letter which starts at the end of one word and ends at the beginning of the next word.

For example:

"The rain in Spain stays mainly in the plain."

Can you see the word '**era**' which starts at the end of 'The' and ends at the beginning of 'rain'?

*Th**e ra**in in Spain stays mainly in the plain.*

Can you spot the 4-letter word hidden in this one?

"We wish you a merry Christmas and a happy new year!"

Can you see the word '**sand**' which starts at the end of 'Christmas' and ends in the word 'and'?

*We wish you a merry Christma**s and** a happy new year!*

"Rain, rain, go away! Come again another day."

Can you see the word '**herd**' which starts at the end of 'another' and ends at the start of 'day'?

*Rain, rain, go away! Come again anot**her d**ay.*

Find a 4-letter word in this quote from Shakespeare's *Macbeth*:

"When shall we three meet again? In thunder, lightning, or in rain?"

Can you see the word '**hens**' which starts at the end of 'When' and ends at the start of 'shall'?

*W**hen s**hall we three meet again?*

HIDDEN WORDS

- Check **how many** letters the question says the word you are looking for is.
- Take each pair of words in turn.
- Imagine you have a magnifying glass that exact number of letters long.
- Imagine hovering the magnifying glass over the words until you spot the hidden word.
- For example: If you are looking for a 3-letter word between: **words until**
- Try: words until   *[dsu = NOT A WORD]*
- Then: words until   *[sun = A WORD]*

Find the hidden words between one word and the next. The brackets indicate how many letters are in the hidden word.

The Listeners by Walter de la Mare

1. 'Is there anybody there?' said the Traveller, [3]

2. Knocking on the moonlit door; [3]

3. And his horse in the silence champed the grasses

   Of the forest's ferny floor:

   And a bird flew up out of the turret, [4]

4. Above the Traveller's head: [3]

5. And he smote upon the door again a second time; [3]

6. 'Is there anybody there?' he said.

   But no one descended to the Traveller; [4]

7. No head from the leaf-fringed sill

   Leaned over and looked into his grey eyes, [4]

8. Where he stood perplexed and still.

   But only a host of phantom listeners [3]

9. That dwelt in the lone house then [3]

10. Stood listening in the quiet of the moonlight

To that voice from the world of men:

Stood thronging the faint moonbeams on the dark stair, [4]

11.   That goes down to the empty hall,

Hearkening in an air stirred and shaken

By the lonely Traveller's call.

And he felt in his heart their strangeness, [5]

12. Their stillness answering his cry,

While his horse moved, cropping the dark turf,

'Neath the starred and leafy sky;

For he suddenly smote on the door, even [3]

13.   Louder, and lifted his head:—

'Tell them I came, and no one answered, [4]

14.   That I kept my word,' he said.

Never the least stir made the listeners,

Though every word he spake

Fell echoing through the shadowiness of the still house [5]

15.   From the one man left awake:

Ay, they heard his foot upon the stirrup,

And the sound of iron on stone,

And how the silence surged softly backward,

When the plunging hoofs were gone. [3]

If there is more than one answer and you got only one answer, then you still get the mark.

1.   'Is there anybody there?' said t**he T**raveller, [3]

2.   Knocking on t**he m**oonlit door; [3]

3.   And his horse in the silence champed the grasses

Of the forest's ferny floor:

And a bird flew u**p out** of the turret, [4]

4.   Abo**ve t**he Traveller**'s he**ad: [3]

5.   And he smote upon the doo**r ag**ain a second time; [3]

6.   'Is there anybody there?' he said.

But **no on**e descended to the Traveller; [4]

7.   No head from the leaf-fringed sill

Leane**d ove**r and looke**d int**o his grey eyes, [4]

8.   Where he stood perplexed and still.

Bu**t on**ly a host of phantom listeners [3]

9.   That dwel**t in** the lone hou**se t**hen [3]

10. Stood listening in the quiet of the moonlight

To that voice from the world of men:

Stood thronging the faint moonbeams on the d**ark s**tair, [4]

11. That goes down to the empty hall,

Hearkening in an air stirred and shaken

By the lonely Traveller's call.

And he felt in his heart t**heir s**trangeness, [5]

12. Their stillness answering his cry,

While his horse moved, cropping the dark turf,

'Neath the starred and leafy sky;

For he suddenly smote on the do**or, e**ven [3]

13. Louder, and lifted his head:—

'Tell them I ca**me, an**d **no on**e answered, [4]

14. That I kept my word,' he said.

Never the least stir made the listeners,

Though every word he spake

Fell echoing thr**ough t**he shadowiness of the still house

15. From the one man left awake:

Ay, they heard his foot upon the stirrup,

And the sound o**f ir**on on stone,

And how the silence surged softly backward,

When the plunging hoofs wer**e go**ne. [3]

HIDDEN WORDS

In these questions, you must find a 3 letter word hidden at the end of one word and the start of the next.

1. To be, or not to be, that is the question.
A.   To be
B.   not to
C.   be that
D.   that is
E.   the question

2. John had Great Big Waterproof boots on.
A.   John had
B.   had Great
C.   Great Big
D.   Waterproof boots
E.   boots on

3. "Wendy Moira Angela Darling," replied Wendy.
A.   Wendy Moira
B.   Moira Angela
C.   Angela Darling
D.   Darling replied
E.   replied Wendy

4. "Christmas a humbug, uncle!" said Scrooge's nephew.
A.   Christmas a
B.   a humbug
C.   humbug, uncle!
D.   uncle!" said
E.   said Scrooge's

5. Alice said, "I must be shutting up like a telescope."
A.   Alice said
B.   I must
C.   be shutting
D.   up like
E.   a telescope

6. The doctor never so much as moved.
A.   The doctor
B.   doctor never
C.   never so
D.   so much
E.   much as

7. The next he knew, he was dimly aware that his tongue was hurting.
A.   the next
B.   he knew
C.   was dimly
D.   aware that
E.   tongue was

8. "What is REAL?" asked the Rabbit one day.
A.   What is
B.   is REAL
C.   asked the
D.   the Rabbit
E.   One day

9. "Where are you going today?" says Pooh.
A.   Where are
B.   are you
C.   was dimly
D.   going today
E.   says Pooh

10. That's one small step for [a] man, one giant leap for mankind.
A.   That's one
B.   one small
C.   small step
D.   step for
E.   one giant

11. How long is a piece of string?
A.   How long
B.   long is
C.   is a
D.   a piece
E.   of string

12. Where did all the flowers go?
A.   Where did
B.   did all
C.   all the
D.   the flowers
E.   flowers go

1. To be, or not to be, that is the question.
A.   To be
B.   not to
C.   **be t**hat
D.   that is
E.   the question

2. John had Great Big Waterproof boots on.
A.   John had
B.   had Great
C.   Great Big
D.   Waterproof boots
E.   boot**s on**

3. "Wendy Moira Angela Darling," replied Wendy.
A.   Wendy Moira
B.   Moira Angela
C.   Ange**la D**arling
D.   Darling replied
E.   replied Wendy

4. "Christmas a humbug, uncle!" said Scrooge's nephew.
A.   Christmas a
B.   a humbug
C.   humbu**g, un**cle!
D.   uncle!" said
E.   said Scrooge's

5. Alice said, "I must be shutting up like a telescope."
A.   Alice said
B.   I must
C.   be shutting
D.   up like
E.   **a te**lescope

6. The doctor never so much as moved.
A.   The doctor
B.   doctor never
C.   never so
D.   so much
E.   muc**h as**

7. The next he knew, he was dimly aware that his tongue was hurting.
A.   **the n**ext
B.   he knew
C.   was dimly
D.   aware that
E.   tongue was

8. "What is REAL?" asked the Rabbit one day.
A.   What is
B.   is REAL
C.   asked the
D.   **the R**abbit
E.   One day

9. "Where are you going today?" says Pooh:

A.   Wher**e are**e
B.   are you
C.   was dimly
D.   going today
E.   says Pooh

10. That's one small step for [a] man, one giant leap for mankind.
A.   That'**s one**e
B.   one small
C.   small step
D.   step for
E.   one giant

11. How long is a piece of string?
A.   H**ow l**ong
B.   long is
C.   is a
D.   a piece
E.   of string

12. Where did all the flowers go?
A.   Whe**re d**id
B.   did all
C.   all the
D.   the flowers
E.   flowers go

2 LETTERS STAND FOR NUMBERS

In this question-type, numerals are represented by a digit. You are told which numeral is represented by each letter, and you then need to substitute them into a formula.

For example:

> If A = 3, B = 6, C = 8, D = 2, E = 16, what is the answer to this formula written as a letter?
>
> A x B − D = [?]

You can substitute each of those letters with the number it represents.

This becomes:
3 x 6 − 2 = 16

Since you are asked to express the answer as a letter, you must then check back to see that 16 is represented by E.

The answer is therefore: E

If A = 21, B = 35, C = 5, D = 32, E = 9

A + C + E = [?]

You can substitute each of those letters with the number it represents.

This becomes:
21 + 5 + 9 = 35

Since you are asked to express the answer as a letter, you must then check back to see that 35 is represented by B.

The answer is therefore: B

If A = 2, B = 1, C = 7, D = 4, E = 9

D x B x A x B − C = [?]

You can substitute each of those letters with the number it represents.

This becomes:
4 x 1 x 2 x 1 − 7 = 1

Since you are asked to express the answer as a letter, you must then check back to see that 1 is represented by B.

The answer is therefore: B

LETTERS STAND FOR NUMBERS

- Write the numbers above the letters.
- Work out the maths calculation and find the number.
- Don't forget to convert the number back to a letter!

LEARN THE ORDER OF OPERATIONS ("BODMAS")...

- First: work out the calculations which are inside Brackets (B) and Orders such as squares, cubes and roots (O).
- Second: calculate Division (D) and Multiplication (M) from left to right.
- Third: calculate Addition (A) and Subtraction (S) from left to right.
- Remember the order by learning 'B-O-D-M-A-S'.

'ORDERS'

- A square number is a number multiplied by itself. '3 squared' is written as 3^2. It equals $3 \times 3 = 9$.

- A cube number is a number multiplied by itself and multiplied by itself again. '3 cubed' is written as 3^3. It equals $3 \times 3 \times 3 = 27$.

'PRODUCTS' AND 'SUMS'

- The 'product' of some numbers is the answer when you multiply those numbers together. For example, the product of 3 and 2 is 6 ($3 \times 2 = 6$).

- The 'sum' of some numbers is the answer when you add those numbers together. For example, the sum of 3 and 2 is 5 ($3 + 2 = 5$).

What is the answer to these number sentences?

1.   If A = 2, B = 1, C = 7, D = 4, E = 14

D ÷ B + A + B + C = [?]

Mark your answer below:

A   B   C   D   (E)

2.   If A = 1, B = 2, C = 3, D = 4, E = 5

B^3 − D + A = [?]

Mark your answer below:

A   B   C   D   (E)

3.   If A = 2, B = 4, C = 6, D = 8, E = 10

E − C + A = [?]

Mark your answer below:

A   B   (C)   D   E

4. If A = 25, B = 10, C = 70, D = 50, E = 2

   A x B ÷ D x E = [?]

   Mark your answer below:

   A (B) C D E

5. If A = 9, B = 8, C = 7, D = 6, E = 5

   A − B + E = [?]

   Mark your answer below:

   A B C (D) E

6. If A = 2, B = 1, C = 7, D = 4, E = 9

   (D − B) x (A + B) = [?]

   Mark your answer below:

   A B C D (E)

7. If A = 0, B = 5, C = 6, D = 2, E = 1

   Subtract the product of 2E and B from the sum of C and 2D.

   Mark your answer below:

   (A) B C D E

8. If A = -3, B = 10, C = 7, D = 4, E = 9

   $A + E + D = [\ ?\ ]$

   Mark your answer below:

   A (B) C D E

9. If A = 25, B = 5, C = 50, D = 10, E = 3

   $(D - B)^2 \times E - C = [\ ?\ ]$

   Mark your answer below:

   (A) B C D E

10. If A = 2, B = 4, C = 7, D = 3, E = 5

    $E^2 - B^2 = [\ ?\ ]^2$

    Mark your answer below:

    A B C (D) E

11. If A = 8, B = 12, C = 100, D = 9, E = 120

    $D \times B - A = [\ ?\ ]$

    Mark your answer below:

    A B (C) D E

12. If A = 14, B = 6, C = 7, D = 144, E = 12

$\sqrt{D} \div B + E = [\ ?\ ]$

Mark your answer below:

(A) B C D E

13. If A = 30, B = 15, C = 5, D = 3, E = 2

$A \div E \times D \div C \div D = [\ ?\ ]$

Mark your answer below:

A B C (D) E

14. If A = -12, B = 6, C = 3, D = 4, E = 5

$A + B + C + D + E = [\ ?\ ]$

Mark your answer below:

A (B) C D E

15. If A = 10, B = 1, C = 5, D = 4, E = 2

$A - D - B = [\ ?\ ]$

Mark your answer below:

A B (C) D E

23

1. If A = 2, B = 1, C = 7, D = 4, E = 14

    D ÷ B + A + B + C = [?]

    Mark your answer below:

    A   B   C   D   **E**

2. If A = 1, B = 2, C = 3, D = 4, E = 5

    B^3 − D + A = [?]

    Mark your answer below:

    A   B   C   D   **E**

3. If A = 2, B = 4, C = 6, D = 8, E = 10

    E − C + A = [?]

    Mark your answer below:

    A   B   **C**   D   E

4. If A = 25, B = 10, C = 70, D = 50, E = 2

   A x B ÷ D x E = [?]

   Mark your answer below:

   A **B** C D E

5. If A = 9, B = 8, C = 7, D = 6, E = 5

   A − B + E = [?]

   Mark your answer below:

   A B C **D** E

6. If A = 2, B = 1, C = 7, D = 4, E = 9

   (D − B) x (A + B) = [?]

   Mark your answer below:

   A B C D **E**

7. If A = 0, B = 5, C = 6, D = 2, E = 1

   Subtract the product of 2E and B from the sum of C and 2D.

   Mark your answer below:

   A B C D E

8. If A = -3, B = 10, C = 7, D = 4, E = 9

   A + E + D = [?]

   Mark your answer below:

   A   **B**   C   D   E

9. If A = 25, B = 5, C = 50, D = 10, E = 3

   $(D - B)^2 \times E - C = [?]$

   Mark your answer below:

   A   B   C   D   E

10. If A = 2, B = 4, C = 7, D = 3, E = 5

    $E^2 - B^2 = [?]^2$

    Mark your answer below:

    A   B   C   **D**   E

11. If A = 8, B = 12, C = 100, D = 9, E = 120

    D x B − A = [?]

    Mark your answer below:

    A   B   **C**   D   E

12. If A = 14, B = 6, C = 7, D = 144, E = 12

$\sqrt{D} \div B + E = [\ ?\ ]$

Mark your answer below:

A   B   C   D   E

13. If A = 30, B = 15, C = 5, D = 3, E = 2

$A \div E \times D \div C \div D = [\ ?\ ]$

Mark your answer below:

A   B   C   **D**   E

14. If A = -12, B = 6, C = 3, D = 4, E = 5

$A + B + C + D + E = [\ ?\ ]$

Mark your answer below:

A   **B**   C   D   E

15. If A = 10, B = 1, C = 5, D = 4, E = 2

$A - D - B = [\ ?\ ]$

Mark your answer below:

A   B   **C**   D   E

3 MOVE A LETTER TO MAKE A NEW WORD

In this question-type, you are given two words. You must take one letter out of the first word and insert it into the next word, making sure that after the move, both the new first word and the new second word make sense. You are not allowed to move any of the other letters.

For example:

pears   and

*Take out the '**s**' from 'pears' (leaving the new word 'pear') and add the 's' to the start of 'and' (to make the new word '**s**and').*

pears   **s**and   .

Try:

flare   pay

*Take out the '**l**' from 'flare' (leaving the new word 'fare') and insert the 'l' as the new second letter of 'pay' (to make the new word 'p**l**ay').*

flare   play

hopping   hone

*Take out the '**p**' from 'hopping' (leaving the new word 'hoping') and insert the 'p' as the new first letter of 'hone' (to make the new word '**p**hone').*

hopping   **p**hone

raft   light

*Take out the '**f**' from 'raft' (leaving the new word 'rat') and insert the 'f' as the new first letter of 'light' (to make the new word '**f**light').*

raft   **f**light

chain   bit

*Take out the '**a**' from 'chain' (leaving the new word 'chin') and insert the 'a' as the new second letter of 'bit' (to make the new word 'b**a**it').*

chain   b**a**it

Your turn ☺

Move one letter from the first word to the second word, to make two new words.

Write the new words out.

1. bout   curt   _____ + _____

2. traced   seal   _____ + _____

3. grate   gown   _____ + _____

4. praise   bred   _____ + _____

5. stray   anger   _____ + _____

6. float   hop   _____ + _____

7. insert   cow   _____ + _____

8. learning too   _____ + _____

9. especial spar   _____ + _____

10. print bid _____ + _____

11. bear arrow _____ + _____

12. cube risk _____ + _____

13. petal over _____ + _____

14. flour sow _____ + _____

15. fearful ate _____ + _____

16. below far _____ + _____

17. wage fan _____ + _____

18. weight son _____ + _____

19. theirs tool _____ + _____

20. chill lose _____ + _____

21. brush beach _____ + _____

22. holly cot _____ + _____

1. bout   curt
but / court

2. traced seal
raced / steal

3. grate   gown
gate / grown

4. praise bred
prise / bread

5. stray   anger
stay / ranger

6. float   hop
flat / hoop

7. insert cow
inset / crow

8. learning   too
earning / tool

9. especial   spar
special/spear/spare

10. print   bid
pint / bird

11. bear   arrow
ear / barrow

12. cube   risk
cue / brisk

13. petal over
peal / overt

14. flour sow
four / slow

15. fearful   ate
earful / fate

16. below   far
blow / fear/fare

17. wage   fan
age / fawn

18. weight son
eight / sown

19. theirs tool
their / tools/stool

20. chill   lose
hill / close

21. brush beach
bush / breach

22. holly   cot
holy / colt/clot

4 ANALOGIES / CONNECTIONS

In this question-type, you need to notice connections between different words and use that connection to make up a 'rule' that will enable you to find another word with the same connection.

Here are some examples of analogies:

> Hexagon is to SIX as octagon is to _____.

How are 'hexagon' and 'SIX' connected?
A hexagon has SIX sides.

Use this connection to make up a sentence for the analogy.

An octagon has _____ sides.

An octagon has EIGHT sides.

> **SO:** Hexagon is to SIX as octagon is to EIGHT.

Web is to WEAVE as story is to _____.

How are 'web' and 'WEAVE' connected?

You WEAVE a web.

Use this connection to make up a sentence for the analogy.

You _____ a story.

You TELL a story.

SO: Web is to WEAVE as story is to TELL.

Toe is to FOOT as finger is to _____.

How are 'toe' and 'FOOT' connected?

A toe is at the end of the FOOT.

Use this connection to make up a sentence for the analogy.

A finger is at the end of a _____.

A finger is at the end of a HAND.

SO: Toe is to FOOT as finger is to HAND.

In each case, you have to make up a sentence which explains the connection between the two words. Then use that same sentence structure to find the missing word.

Try this:

England is to ENGLISH as France is to _____.

How are 'England' and ENGLISH connected?

In England, people speak ENGLISH.

Use this connection to make up a sentence for the analogy.

In France, people speak _____.

In France, people speak FRENCH.

SO: England is to ENGLISH as France is to FRENCH.

Sometimes, you have to choose two words. For example:

Tall is to (SHORT / OLD / TWO) as high is to (LOW / THIN / ONE).

Make up a sentence:

Tall is the opposite of SHORT.
High is the opposite of LOW.

So the answer is 'SHORT' and 'LOW'.

Your turn ☺

Choose one word only from each pair of brackets to complete the sentence.

1. Fly is to (INSECT / HELICOPTER / PILOT) as
    float is to (SAILOR / BOAT / SEALION).

2. Drink is to (WATER / WET / DRY) as
    eat is to (DELICIOUS / FOOD / COOKED).

3. Stripe is to (GIRAFFE / ZEBRA / LION) as
    spot is to (LEOPARD / ELEPHANT / PENGUIN).

4. Follow is to (ALUMINIUM / COPPER / LEAD) as
    open is to (NEAR / CLOSE / ADJACENT).

5. Colour is to (YELLOW / DRAW / FAVOURITE) as
    animal is to (ALIVE / FRIENDLY / DOG).

6. Hand is to (FOOT / GLOVE / HELMET) as
    neck is to (SCARF / SOCK / CHIN).

7. Brave is to (COWARDLY / FEARLESS / HAPPY) as
    cheerful is to (HUNGRY / MISERABLE / OLD).

8. Pen is to (SPELL / READ / WRITE) as
    scissors is to (DECORATE / CUT / SHARP).

9. Club is to (GOLF / BOOK / FOOTBALL) as
    racquet is to (TENNIS / PLAY / NOISE).

1. Fly is to (INSECT / **HELICOPTER** / PILOT) as
    float is to (SAILOR / **BOAT** / SEALION).

A HELICOPTER <u>flies</u> in the air.
A BOAT <u>floats</u> in the water.

2. Drink is to (**WATER** / WET / DRY) as
    eat is to (DELICIOUS / **FOOD** / COOKED).

You <u>drink</u> WATER.
You <u>eat</u> FOOD.

3. Stripe is to (GIRAFFE / **ZEBRA** / LION) as
    spot is to (**LEOPARD** / ELEPHANT / PENGUIN).

A ZEBRA has <u>stripes</u>.
A LEOPARD has <u>spots</u>.

4. Follow is to (ALUMINIUM / COPPER / **LEAD**) as
    open is to (NEAR / **CLOSE** / ADJACENT).

<u>Follow</u> is the opposite of LEAD.
<u>Open</u> is the opposite of CLOSE.

5.	Colour is to (**YELLOW** / DRAW / FAVOURITE) as
	animal is to (ALIVE / FRIENDLY / **DOG**).

YELLOW is a <u>colour</u>.
A DOG is an <u>animal</u>.

6.	Hand is to (FOOT / **GLOVE** / HELMET) as
	neck is to (**SCARF** / SOCK / CHIN).

You wear a GLOVE on your <u>hand</u>.
You wear a SCARF on your <u>neck</u>.

7.	Brave is to (**COWARDLY** / FEARLESS / HAPPY) as
	cheerful is to (HUNGRY / **MISERABLE** / OLD).

<u>Brave</u> is the opposite of COWARDLY.
<u>Cheerful</u> is the opposite of MISERABLE.

8.	Pen is to (SPELL / READ / **WRITE**) as
	scissors is to (DECORATE / **CUT** / SHARP).

You use a <u>pen</u> to WRITE.
You use <u>scissors</u> to CUT.

9.	Club is to (**GOLF** / BOOK / FOOTBALL) as
	racquet is to (**TENNIS** / PLAY / NOISE).

You play GOLF with a golf <u>club</u>.
You play TENNIS with a tennis <u>racquet</u>.

5 LOGIC QUESTIONS

In this question-type, you need to read information carefully and use it to answer a question. You often need to work through several steps and read through a number of times to get to the answer.

For example:

Four friends are talking about their favourite pet animals. Jason likes all animals. Helen hates dogs but likes all other pets. Amara likes cats best but also likes fish. Safira has a pet hamster but wishes it were a cat. **How many of the friends like cats?**

Does Jason like cats? Yes – he likes 'all animals'.
Does Helen like cats? Yes – she doesn't like dogs, but she likes all other pets so must like cats.
Does Amara like cats? Yes, it says 'Amara likes cats best'.
Does Safira like cats? Yes, this is implied by the fact that she wishes her pet hamster were a cat.
Answer: All four of the friends like cats.

Eloise wanted to have a party. She asked her family when the best day would be. Mum wants it to be at the weekend. Dad is busy on weekdays. Her sister says she will only come to the party if it is on a day beginning with S. Her brother is going on holiday between Tuesday and Saturday. On what day can Eloise have the party to suit everyone?

Go through each person and work out the days they can do. It might be useful to write down the days of the week and cross them off as and when you can eliminate them:

Mum: only Saturday or Sunday (because she wants it to be the weekend).
Dad: only Saturday or Sunday (because he is busy on weekdays – i.e. Monday to Friday).
Sister: only Saturday or Sunday (because these are the only days beginning with an S).
Brother: only Sunday or Monday (because he is on holiday between Tuesday and Saturday).

Sunday, ~~Monday, Tuesday, Wednesday, Thursday, Friday, Saturday~~

<u>Answer</u>: That leaves Sunday as the only day which suits all the family's preferences.

LOGIC QUESTIONS

- You may be given irrelevant information. Before reading all the facts, go straight to the question so that you know which information is going to be relevant.
- Eliminate anything that you know is not the answer, and then go back to see what possible answers are left.
- You usually have to read through the information at least twice.

ANNOTATE THE INFORMATION

- Think about how you can annotate the information given to avoid you having to write everything out again. For example:
- You could circle possible answers, add a tally above people's/objects' names, and cross out those which you can eliminate.

Logic Questions

1. Flavio, Joshua, Jilly and Aidan are having a special lunch. For the first course, they can choose between chicken soup and an avocado tower. For the main course, they could have either lamb with potatoes or macaroni cheese. For dessert, they can choose strawberry ice cream or hot treacle pudding.

    Flavio likes all his food to be hot but can't stand cheese.
    Joshua and Jilly are vegetarian.
    Aidan doesn't like avocado but loves cheese.
    Joshua and Aidan like both ice cream and hot treacle pudding.

    How many children eat lamb?

2. Grant and Matt are studying Geography and Maths. Serren and Greg are learning French and Maths. Matt and Greg are studying History and Spanish.

    Who is studying French but not Spanish?

3. Shalina, Alex and Tatiana went to the theme park. Shalina and Alex went on the log flume while Tatiana decided to go on the pirate ship instead. Tatiana and Shalina enjoyed the dodgems but Alex didn't like the way people bumped into her. Shalina went on the helter skelter by herself whilst Alex and Tatiana went to get some doughnuts. Shalina bought three ice creams: one each. Tatiana went home before the others went on the biggest roller-coaster in the park.

Who went on the log flume, dodgems and roller-coaster? Choose from one of the following options:

A. Shalina
B. Alex
C. Tatiana
D. Shalina and Alex
E. Shalina and Tatiana

4. Latin is a language. Every language is a means of communication.

Based only on the statements above, which of the following is logically true?:

A. Most people in the world communicate using Latin.
B. Most people don't know Latin.
C. Every language is Latin.
D. Latin was spoken by the Romans.
E. Latin is a means of communication.

Answers to Logic Questions

1. How many children eat lamb?

   One. Only Flavio eats lamb. We know that he eats lamb because he 'can't stand cheese' and the alternative to lamb is 'macaroni cheese'. We know Joshua and Jilly do not eat lamb because they 'are vegetarian'. We know Aidan chooses the macaroni cheese instead of the lamb because he 'loves cheese'.

2. Who is studying French but not Spanish?

   Serren.

3. Who went on the log flume, dodgems and roller-coaster?

   D. Shalina and Alex.

4. Latin is a language. Every language is a means of communication.
Based only on the statements above, which is logically true?:

   E. Latin is a means of communication. *Note, the question asks you to base the information ONLY on the statements above, not on your own knowledge or opinions.*

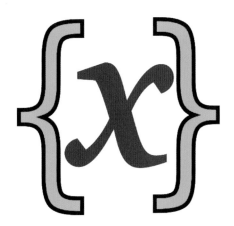

6 MAKE THE WORD IN BRACKETS

In this question-type, you are given a 'worked example' made up of three words, one of which is in brackets. The word in brackets has been created using a particular combination of letters from the other two words. Once you work out the combination in the worked example, you can apply this combination to complete another group of words where the word in brackets is missing.

For example:

        tax [rat] rib   tub [???] bed

The first word in brackets ('rat') has been created as follows:

R: the <u>first</u> letter of the <u>second</u> word +
A: the <u>second</u> letter of the <u>first</u> word +
T: the <u>first</u> letter of the <u>first</u> word.

Combine the letters in the second group in the same way to find the missing word (???):

B: the <u>first</u> letter of the <u>second</u> word +
U: the <u>second</u> letter of the <u>first</u> word +
T: the <u>first</u> letter of the <u>first</u> word.

Another example:

allow [watch] sketch   types [?????] swamp

The first word in brackets ('watch') has been created as follows:

W: the fifth letter of the first word +
A: the first letter of the first word +
TCH: the last three letters of the second word.

This means that the missing word in the second group of words (?????) will be created as follows:

S: the fifth letter of the first word +
T: the first letter of the first word +
AMP: the last three letters of the second word.

Another example:

half [love] oven   fast [????] hope

The first word in brackets ('love') has been created as follows:

L: the third letter of the first word +
OVE: the first three letters of the second word.

This means that the missing word (????) will be as follows:

S: the third letter of the first word +
HOP: the first three letters of the second word.

Sometimes the question will be more difficult because there is a variety of different ways in which the word in brackets could have been created. You then need to try each way to see which combination works to create the missing word. For example:

belong [clean] cinema   larder [?????] chrism

The first word in brackets is 'clean' which has been created by:

C: The first letter of the second word +
L: The third letter of the first word +
E: EITHER the second letter of the first word OR the fourth letter of the second word +
A: The last letter of the second word +
N: EITHER The fifth letter of the first word OR the third letter of the second word.

This means that the missing word could be:

C: The first letter of the second word +
R: The third letter of the first word +
A or I: Either the second letter of the first word or the fourth letter of the second word +
M: The last letter of the second word +
E or R: Either the fifth letter of the first word or the third letter of the second word.

This means the missing word is one of the following:
CRAME / CRIME / CRAMR / CRIMR

Of the above possibilities, only 'CRIME' is a real word.

1. unit [bait] bake   sage [????] rate

2. pour [pram] lamb   soap [????] lots

3. gift [grit] area   pear [????] test

4. crop [clog] goal   moan [????] time

5. short [ghost] wrong   crime [????] steep

6. hover [drove] sword   vinyl [?????] bonus

7. graze [same] amuse   shout [????] moths

8. sharp [spar] sweep   colds [????] house

9. church [rush] census   staged [????] banana

10. focus [horse] other   rabid [?????] Japan

11. spell [sleep] quell   gnarl [?????] stirs

12. post [too] stop   bear [???] mode

13. sweet [west] hotel   opera [????] aptly

1. unit [bait] bake   sage [rage] rate

2. pour [pram] lamb   soap [spot] lots

3. gift [grit] area   pear [peer] test

4. crop [clog] goal   moan [meat] time

5. short [ghost] wrong   crime [price] steep

6. hover [drove] sword   vinyl [sunny] bonus

7. graze [same] amuse   shout [hoot] moths

8. sharp [spar] sweep   colds [held] house

9. church [rush] census   staged [gnat] banana

10. focus [horse] other   rabid [panda] Japan

11. spell [sleep] quell   gnarl [grain] stirs

12. post [too] stop   bear [red OR ode] mode

13. sweet [west] hotel   opera [plot] aptly

7 WORD WITHIN A WORD

In this question-type, you are given a sentence where one word is incomplete: it has had three consecutive letters taken out. The three consecutive letters together make up a separate word. You have to find the three-letter word that would slot in anywhere in the incomplete word to complete it.

For example:
Don't **ST** crying.

A) TAR   B) ART   C) EAR   D) ARE   E) IRE

The answer is B) <u>ART</u>

Don't **ST**<u>ART</u> *crying. [Even though 'ARE' could have made the new word 'STARE', it wouldn't have made sense in the sentence (Don't STARE crying).]*

The **FN** furrowed her brow.

A) ROW   B) OWN   C) LOW   D) RAM   E) EAR

The answer is A) ROW

The **F**<u>ROW</u>**N** *furrowed her brow. [Even though 'LOW' could have made the new word 'FLOWN', it wouldn't have made sense in the sentence (The FLOWN furrowed her brow).]*

It was hard to **PI** the ship in the bad weather.

A) RAT   B) LAT   C) LOT   D) SIT   E) HAD

The answer is C) <u>LOT</u>

It was hard to **PI**<u>LOT</u> the ship in the bad weather.

The wedding cake had five **LRS**.

A) LAY   B) YEA   C) EAR   D) AYE   E) ORE

The answer is D) <u>AYE</u>

The wedding cake had five **L**<u>AYE</u>**RS**.

During the holidays, the **CHERS** set lots of homework.

A) TAR   B) TEA   C) APE   D) ARE   E) LOP

The answer is B) <u>TEA</u>

During the holidays, the <u>TEA</u>**CHERS** set lots of homework.

The main **TE** of fairytales is the triumph of good over evil.

A) AIM   B) BET   C) HAT   D) HAM   E) HEM

The answer is E) <u>HEM</u>

The main **T**<u>HEM</u>**E** of fairytales is the triumph of good over evil.

- First, read the sentence and see whether you can guess the missing word. This will save a lot of time if so.

- If you can guess the word, work out which letters are missing and then look for those letters amongst the multiple choice answers.

- If you can't guess the word, go through each of the possible answers systematically to place them at the beginning, middle and end of the incomplete word to see which one both makes a new word.

- Don't forget to re-read the sentence at the end to check you have chosen an appropriate word.

- If you have time to check your answer, write out the new spelling to check that you have chosen the correct combination of letters to complete the word.

1. A cuboid is a three-DISIONAL shape.

A) MEN   B) AGE   C) RAG   D) AGE   E) CUB

2. The LOWNERS allowed us to camp on their land.

A) OWN   B) FUN   C) AND   D) FAR   E) TIE

3. Roman ARCECTURE is beautiful.

A) SIT   B) ART   C) NIT   D) BIT   E) HIT

4. I wouldn't bother you, but it's IMPORT.

A) TAN   B) BUG   C) BIG   D) ATE   E) RAN

5. IGANCE of the law is no excuse.

A) ART   B) NOR   C) MAN   D) END   E) ROD

6. There were several CIDATES for the job.

A) DID   B) ATE   C) AND   D) EAT   E) OAT

7.   The train DUCTOR checked everyone's tickets.

A) TOR   B) COT   C) CON   D) RAN   E) WAN

8.   The boy always travelled by public TSPORT.

A) AIR   B) RAN   C) TUB   D) FIR   E) RAT

9.   If they need more details, you can EORATE on the point.

A) FED   B) AIR   C) LAB   D) PEN   E) PER

10.   That point has no RELECE to the matter in hand.

A) ICE   B) ACE   C) AIL   D) VAN   E) MAR

11.   Jane Austen wrote a book called *Pride and PREJUD*.

A) GEM   B) ACE   C) ICE   D) USE   E) IRE

12.   She said it was AMUOUS because there was more than one interpretation.

A) AIR   B) TIN   C) BIG   D) OUR   E) ICE

13.   The LANDSE was mountainous.

A) HEN   B) HAT   C) CAP   D) CAR   E) CAB

1.   A cuboid is a three-DI MEN SIONAL shape.

A) MEN   B) AGE   C) RAG   D) AGE   E) CUB

2.   The L AND OWNERS allowed us to camp on their land.

A) OWN   B) FUN   C) AND   D) FAR   E) TIE

3.   Roman ARC HIT ECTURE is beautiful.

A) SIT   B) ART   C) NIT   D) BIT   E) HIT

4.   I wouldn't bother you, but it's IMPOR TAN T.

A) TAN   B) BUG   C) BIG   D) ATE   E) RAN

5.   IG NOR ANCE of the law is no excuse.

A) ART   B) NOR   C) MAN   D) END   E) ROD

6.   There were several C AND IDATES for the job.

A) DID   B) ATE   C) AND   D) EAT   E) OAT

7. The train CON DUCTOR checked everyone's tickets.

A) TOR   B) COT   C) CON   D) RAN   E) WAN

8. The boy always travelled by public T RAN SPORT.

A) AIR   B) RAN   C) TUB   D) FIR   E) RAT

9. If they need more details, you can E LAB ORATE on the point.

A) FED   B) AIR   C) LAB   D) PEN   E) PER

10. That point has no RELE VAN CE to the matter in hand.

A) ICE   B) ACE   C) AIL   D) VAN   E) MAR

11. Jane Austen wrote a book called *Pride and PREJUD ICE*.

A) GEM   B) ACE   C) ICE   D) USE   E) IRE

12. She said it was AM BIG UOUS because there was more than one interpretation.

A) AIR   B) TIN   C) BIG   D) OUR   E) ICE

13. The LANDS CAP E was mountainous.

A) HEN   B) HAT   C) CAP   D) CAR   E) CAB

8 LETTER PAIRS

In this question-type, you have to work out the connection between two letter pairs, and apply it to work out a missing letter pair. If the alphabet is not already written out for you, it might help to write it out. Make sure you know all 26 letters of the alphabet off by heart and can write them out accurately, to avoid mistakes. You can also draw lines to show the connection, as below.

For example:

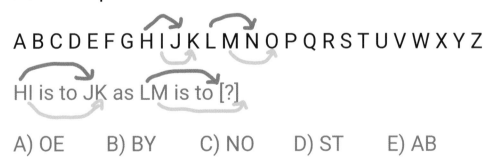

A) OE   B) BY   C) NO   D) ST   E) AB

The answer is C) <u>NO</u>

You know this because to get from H to J, you have to go two letters to the right. To get from I to K, you have to go two letters to the right. So you do the same with L and M.

For example:

BG is to DI as RW is to [?]

A) MB   B) DE   C) NO   D) TY   E) AB

The answer is D) <u>TY</u>

You know this because to get from B to D, you have to go two letters to the right. To get from G to I, you have to go two letters to the right. So you do the same with R and W.

Sometimes, the connection is a 'mirror image'. The mid-point of the alphabet is between M and N, and sometimes you have to imagine a mirror there, although the mirror line could be elsewhere:

AB is to ZY as CD is to [?]   The answer is A) <u>XW</u>

You know this because A is 13 letters away from the mid-point, so you count 13 letters away from the mid-point in the other direction, which gets you to Z. B is 12 letters away from the mid-point, so you count 12 letters away from the mid-point in the other direction, which gets you to Y. If you find the mirror image letter of C, which is 11 letters away from the mid-point, you will get X, which is 11 letters away in the other direction. D is 10 letters away from the mid-point, so its pair is W, 10 letters away on the other side.

Sometimes, the gap between the first letters in the pair is different to the gap between the second letters in each pair:

A B C D E F G H I J K L M N O P Q R S T U V W X Y Z

JM is to LP as RU is to [?]

A) XU   B) TU   C) ST   D) TX   E) LN

The answer is D) <u>TX</u>

Here, to find the second pair, you 'add' (= go right) two letters to the first letter, and add three letters to the second letter.

You could also find an example where the first letter goes in the opposite direction to the second letter:

A B C D E F G H I J K L M N O P Q R S T U V W X Y Z

LM is to JP as TU is to [?]

A) XU   B) TU   C) TX   D) RX   E) LN

The answer is D) <u>RX</u>

Here, to find the second pair, you 'subtract' (= go left) two letters to the first letter, and 'add' (= go right) three letters to the second letter.

LETTER PAIRS

- Think of each letter separately:
  - The <u>first</u> letter in the first pair will be connected to the <u>first</u> letter in the second pair;
  - The <u>second</u> letter in the first pair will be connected to the <u>second</u> letter in the second pair;
  - And so on!

- Don't forget that some patterns will have the letters going backwards, and others will have the letters going forwards, whilst others will be mirror image.

- Imagine the alphabet as a loop. If you need to go left of 'A', then the next letter will be 'Z'.

A B C D E F G H I J K L M N O P Q R S T U V W X Y Z

1.   GJ is to OR as AD is to [?].

A) IM   B) PQ   C) IL   D) VW   E) WZ

A B C D E F G H I J K L M N O P Q R S T U V W X Y Z

2.   JK is to OH as AB is to [?].

A) IM   B) PQ   C) FY   D) VW   E) WZ

A B C D E F G H I J K L M N O P Q R S T U V W X Y Z

3.   AC is to DF as NP is to [?].

A) JM   B) QS   C) IS   D) SQ   E) QL

A B C D E F G H I J K L M N O P Q R S T U V W X Y Z

4.   MN is to LO as KJ is to [?].

A) IN   B) PQ   C) PR   D) QR   E) QP

A B C D E F G H I J K L M N O P Q R S T U V W X Y Z

5.   VW is to SV as KL is to [?].

A) IK   B) HL   C) KH   D) HK   E) GL

A B C D E F G H I J K L M N O P Q R S T U V W X Y Z

6.   ABC is to HIJ as NOP is to [?].

A) TUV   B) UVW   C) STU   D) VWX   E) WXY

A B C D E F G H I J K L M N O P Q R S T U V W X Y Z

7.   AZY is to VUT as PON is to [?].

A) IHG   B) JKL   C) KJI   D) LKJ   E) IJK

A B C D E F G H I J K L M N O P Q R S T U V W X Y Z

8.   ADG is to ZWT as BEH is to [?].

A) VUT   B) RST   C) YVS   D) SVY   E) ZYX

A B C D E F G H I J K L M N O P Q R S T U V W X Y Z

9.   KMC is to GOB as PTH is to [?].

A) BAT   B) HIT   C) LVG   D) LWB   E) ZYX

A B C D E F G H I J K L M N O P Q R S T U V W X Y Z

1.   GJ is to OR as AD is to [?]. [+ 8 for both letters]

A) IM   B) PQ   C) IL   D) VW   E) WZ

A B C D E F G H I J K L M N O P Q R S T U V W X Y Z

2.   JK is to OH as AB is to [?]. [+ 5 then − 3]

A) IM   B) PQ   C) FY   D) VW   E) WZ

A B C D E F G H I J K L M N O P Q R S T U V W X Y Z

3.   AC is to DF as NP is to [?]. [+ 3 for both letters]

A) JM   B) QS   C) IS   D) SQ   E) QL

A B C D E F G H I J K L M N O P Q R S T U V W X Y Z

4.   MN is to LO as KJ is to [?]. [a mirror line between M and N]

A) IN   B) PQ   C) PR   D) QR   E) QP

A B C D E F G H I J K L M N O P Q R S T U V W X Y Z

5.   VW is to SV as KL is to [?]. [- 3, - 1]

A) IK   B) HL   C) KH   D) HK   E) GL

A B C D E F G H I J K L M N O P Q R S T U V W X Y Z

6.   ABC is to HIJ as NOP is to [?]. [+ 7 for each letter]

A) TUV   B) UVW   C) STU   D) VWX   E) WXY

A B C D E F G H I J K L M N O P Q R S T U V W X Y Z

7.   AZY is to VUT as PON is to [?]. [-5 for each letter]

A) IHG   B) JKL   C) KJI   D) LKJ   E) IJK

A B C D E F G H I J K L M N O P Q R S T U V W X Y Z

8.   ADG is to ZWT as BEH is to [?]. [mirror line between M and N]

A) VUT   B) RST   C) YVS   D) SVY   E) ZYX

A B C D E F G H I J K L M N O P Q R S T U V W X Y Z

9.   KMC is to GOB as PTH is to [?]. [-4, +2, -1]

A) BAT   B) HIT   C) LVG   D) LWB   E) ZYX

9 CLOSEST IN MEANING

In this question-type, you have to choose two words that are closest in meaning to each other. You must choose one word from each set of brackets. They should be the same word-class (i.e., a noun must match with a noun, a verb with a verb, etc) and should be synonyms which are as close in meaning as possible.

For example:

(confession, admission, rejection)   (entry, exit, worry)

'Admission' to the cinema means 'entry' to the cinema.

(cooperation, joke, fly)   (good, work, teamwork)

'Cooperation' means working together with someone else = 'teamwork'.

(sanctuary, release, rescue)   (option, safety, hope)

I sought sanctuary/safety in the church.

Choose the pair of words that are closest in meaning. You must choose one word from each set of brackets.

1.   (hurt, spy, rubbish)   (injure, elbow, destroy)

2.   (treatment, ill, poorly)   (cure, doctor, hospital)

3.   (pile, arrange, open)   (shut, organize, close)

4.   (anxiety, worry, stress)   (hard, dry, emphasis)

5.   (wrong, accurate, vague)   (helpful, precise, justice)

6.   (old, young, youthful)   (elderly, toddler, tall)

7.   (muddy, swampy, damp)   (wet, towel, clean)

8.   (dulcet, singing, voice)   (choir, melodious, sweets)

9.   (documentation, diary, painting)   (biography, paperwork, art)

10. (blue, green, magenta)   (black, crimson, white)

11. (roof, gateway, window)   (kitchen, portal, basement)

12. (coat, hooves, beak)   (arms, fleece, teeth)

1. (hurt, spy, rubbish)   (injure, elbow, destroy)

2. (treatment, ill, poorly)   (cure, doctor, hospital)

3. (pile, arrange, open) (shut, organize, close)

4. (anxiety, worry, stress)   (hard, dry, emphasis)

5. (wrong, accurate, vague) (helpful, precise, justice)

6. (old, young, youthful)   (elderly, toddler, tall)

7. (muddy, swampy, damp) (wet, towel, clean)

8. (dulcet, singing, voice)   (choir, melodious, sweets)

9. (documentation, diary, painting) (biography, paperwork, art)

10. (blue, green, magenta)   (black, crimson, white)

11. (roof, gateway, window) (kitchen, portal, basement)

12. (coat, hooves, beak)   (arms, fleece, teeth)

10 NUMBER SERIES

In this question-type, you are given a series of numbers and have to work out the rule in order to choose the missing number. Sometimes you will need to add or subtract. Other times, you will need to multiply or divide. Sometimes the numbers are connected in a different way, for example, they are all square numbers or triangle numbers. Sometimes there will be a mix of operations, for example, you will have to add and then multiply, or square and then subtract. Sometimes, different rules apply to alternate numbers.

For example:

3, 5, 7, 9, [?]

First, find the rule. The rule is 'add 2' to each term to find the next term. This means the missing number is 11 (which is 9 + 2).

Watch out for questions where this rule is applied to alternate numbers. For example:

1, 3, 1, 5, 1, 7, 1, 9, [?], [?]

The next two numbers will be 1 and 11. This is because the number '1' stays the same and is repeated every other term, and then you 'add 2' to each alternate term.

Sometimes, there is a second pattern relating to the series:

13, 15, 19, 25, 33, 43, [?]
    +2   +4   +6   +8   +10
        +2   +2   +2   +2

Here, there is a second pattern where you add an extra 2 each time. This means that you will add 12 to 43, and the missing number is 55.

Here is one where multiplication is used:

2, 8, 32, 128, [?]

In this series, you multiply the previous term by 4 each time. This means that the missing number is 128 x 4 = 400 + 80 + 32 = 512.

This one uses division:

144, 72, 36, 18, [?]

Here, each term is divided by 2. 18 ÷ 2 = 9, so the missing term is 9.

Imagine if we used subtraction + division + addition:

145, 73, 37, [?]

Here, we 'subtract 1', 'divide by 2' and 'add 1'. So the answer is 19.

This question uses square numbers:

4, 9, 16, 25, [?]

The answer is 36 (6^2 = 6 x 6 = 36). Remember, a square number is any number multiplied by itself.

You could also have a series using prime numbers:

2, 5, 11, 17, [?]

The next number in the series is 23, because the pattern is alternate prime numbers. Remember, a prime number is a number that can only be divided by 1 and itself, i.e. it has no factors other than 1 and itself. 1 does not count as a prime number.

Here, you could add the previous terms together:

3, 4, 7, 11, 18, [?]

3+4 = 7; 4+7 = 11; 7+11=18; 11+18=29, so the answer is 29.

Watch out for two rules being applied to alternate numbers.

1, 2, 4, 4, 9, 8, 16, 16, 25, 32, 36, [?]

1, 2, 4, 4, 9, 8, 16, 16, 25, 32, 36, [?]

Here, we have square numbers alternated by a rule whereby the previous term is doubled. This means that the missing term is double 32, which is 64.

Find the missing number in the series.

1. 3, 6, 9, 12, [?]

2. 1, 3, 6, 10, 15, [?]

3. 1, 2, 6, 24, 120, [?]

4. 5, 20, 10, 40, 15, 60, 20, 80, [?]

5. 29, 27, 25, 23, 21, [?]

6. 13, 17, 25, 41, 73, [?]

7. 7, 23, 14, 24, 21, 25, 28, 26, [?]

8. 1, 2, 3, 2, 4, 6, 3, 6, 9, 4, 8, 12, 5, 10, [?]

9. 250, 200, 150, 100, [?]

10. 13, 17, 19, 23, [?]

11. 14, 18, 20, 24, 30, 31, [?]
Clue: look at this series' similarities with the series in Question 10.

12. 144, 12, 121, 11, 100, 10, [?]

13. 9, 4, -1, -6, [?]

14. -3, 9, -2, 4, -1, 1, 0, 0, 1, 1, 2, 4, 3, [?]

15. 5, 7, 13, 15, 21, 23, 29, [?]

16. 64, 72, 80, 88, [?]

17. 12, 13, 16, 21, 28, 39, 52, [?]

18. 55, 56, 66, 48, 77, 42, [?]

19. 1, 8, 27, 64, [?]

1.   3, 6, 9, 12, [15] (add 3 / 3 times tables)

2.   1, 3, 6, 10, 15, [21] (add one extra each time / triangle numbers)

3.   1, 2, 6, 24, 120, [720] (multiply first term by 2, second term by 3, third term by 4, increasing multiplier by 1 each time)

4.   5, 20, 10, 40, 15, 60, 20, 80, [25, 100] (there are two rules here, firstly, the 5 times table for alternate numbers starting at 5, secondly, add 20 for alternate numbers starting at 20)

5.   29, 27, 25, 23, 21, [19] (take away 2)

6.   13, 17, 25, 41, 73, [137] (double the number you add each time, start by adding 4, then add 8, then add 16, then add 32, then add 64)

7.   7, 23, 14, 24, 21, 25, 28, 26, [35] (two rules: 7 times tables starting with 7 and applying to alternate numbers, then add one each time to alternate numbers starting with 23)

8.   1, 2, 3, 2, 4, 6, 3, 6, 9, 4, 8, 12, 5, 10, [15] (there are three rules here: 1, 2, 3, 4, 5; 2, 4, 6, 8, 10; 3, 6, 9, 12, 15)

9.   250, 200, 150, 100, [50] (subtract 50)

10.   13, 17, 19, 23, [29] (prime numbers)

11.   14, 18, 20, 24, 30, 31, [37] (next prime number + 1)

12.   144, 12, 121, 11, 100, 10, [81] (descending square numbers followed by their square roots)

13.   9, 4, -1, -6, [-11] (subtract 5)

14.   -3, 9, -2, 4, -1, 1, 0, 0, 1, 1, 2, 4, 3, [9] (starting from -3, add 1 for alternate numbers; starting from 9, square the preceding number, e.g. $(-3)^2 = 9$)

15.   5, 7, 13, 15, 21, 23, 29, [31] (+2, +6, alternating pattern)

16.   64, 72, 80, 88, [96] (8 times table)

17.   12, 13, 16, 21, 28, 39, 52, [69] (add increasing prime numbers)

18.   55, 56, 66, 48, 77, 42, [88] (two rules: first rule is increasing 11 times tables for alternate numbers; second rule is decreasing 8 times tables for alternate numbers starting with 56)

19.   1, 8, 27, 64, [125] (next cube number)
Remember, a cube number is a number multiplied by itself and multiplied by itself again, e.g. $1^3 = 1 \times 1 \times 1 = 1$, $2^3 = 2 \times 2 \times 2 = 8$, $3^3 = 3 \times 3 \times 3 = 27$.

WELL DONE FOR COMPLETING THIS VERBAL REASONING BOOK!

LOOK OUT FOR MORE IN THE SERIES:

VERBAL REASONING
NON-VERBAL REASONING
MATHS
ENGLISH

www.fantastichomelearning.com

Printed in Great Britain
by Amazon